Sweeter Than Honey

by LINDSAY LETTERS

HarperOne

*An Imprint of* HarperCollins*Publishers*

Scripture quotations are provided from multiple translations. If no translation is listed, the paraphrase was arranged by the artist.

HarperCollins books may be purchased for educational, business, or sales promotional use. For information, please email the Special Markets Department at SPsales@harpercollins.com.

Cover and campaign photography and styling in collaboration with Laura Kackley / larkphotos.com

FIRST EDITION

ISBN 978-0-06-265145-7

17 18 19 20 21  BRR  10 9 8 7 6 5 4 3 2 1

# HI, friend!

If we could have some time to sit together, over a pretty mug of something yummy or a cold drink over ice, the first thing I would ask you would be this: "Why did you buy this book?" And if you didn't buy it, if you received it as a gift, the first thing I would say to you is "Your friends have excellent taste," and then I would say, "What made you decide to pick up this book and get this far?"

Is it because you thought it was pretty? Because you're super into this coloring book phenomenon? Or hand lettering? Because something on the cover resonated with you? You're searching? You're bored? I wish so badly that we could talk about it, just us two. But since we can't, I'll cut to the chase. You picked up this book because, I believe, the Lord wanted you to. I've just looked on Amazon and there are 1.7 gazillion coloring books for adults. So many incredible choices! Perhaps you have half of them already. But I believe that if something made you pick this book up and get this far into it, God is already starting a work in you, whispering the words "sweet" and "nourish" and "soul" in your ear. Can you hear Him?

I always joke that I don't have a hard time sleeping. A borderline narcoleptic, I really could fall asleep anywhere, anytime. This is because I am, most days, exhausted. As a business owner, mom, overachiever, crazy artist, analytical, ENFP/2, it isn't hard for me to sleep (read: pass out), but it *is* hard for me to *rest*.

How are you at resting? This is a bit of a trick question because the fact that you're choosing to color in your downtime already tells me that you need to be doing something. Gotcha! (This is where, if we were together, we would chuckle and then take another sip, and then sigh.)

When I first started playing around with this book, I asked God what He might allow me to say to you over the course of these pages. Here's what I heard:

## 1. His Word.

I was to letter mostly scripture or words that point to scripture so that you might hear His voice in fresh ways. Please accept these visual aids to the Word of God as His gift to you, to carry with you and treasure for years and years to come. His Word is alive (Hebrews 4:12), **His word is sweeter than honey** (Psalm 119:103), and I pray that you would marvel at how His Word takes on new meaning as you interact with it through coloring.

## 2. His desire to nourish your soul.

God is speaking to you, friend. Telling you to slow down if you're crazy and telling you to wake up if you're bored. Either way, you need nourishment. What do you do after a long day of travel? After a long stretch of sleep? You eat and drink. You nourish your body. You get off your feet and restore yourself so you can get back up and carry on. The words on the following pages were chosen specifically to help you do that. It's my prayer that you would walk away from having spent time on these pages knowing both God and yourself a little bit better, and feeling refreshed and ready to take on whatever is next.

## 3. It's you and me, baby.

As an artist, my most favorite thing about creating art for my store is to birth one piece of work from idea to fruition. I love to take it from a simple idea spark, to a sketch, to a piece of art, to a beautifully styled photo, and then into my customer's hands. That said, the initial idea of creating a coloring book made me feel like the smiling emoji with the sweat drip. Like taking a half-baked roasted vegetable lasagna out of the oven and serving it to my guests! But God gently reminded me that what I was forgetting was you. You! You sweet, beautiful thing with your freshly sharpened pencils or gel pens and ready-creative mind. Without you interacting with these pieces of lettering, they are merely shells. Whether you simply fill in the words in all black or you get after these pages with a flair for color and a rainbow of ammunition, God has gifted you with creativity, and it's what God does in you as you create that truly finishes these pieces.

So what do you say? Are you ready to partner with me in creating beautiful, hand-lettered art in Jesus's holy name? I sure hope so. I'll be praying for you as you do. Praying that many, many hearts find rest and nourishment in a way that only a God as creative and lovely as ours can provide.

XOXO,
Lindsay

**LINDSAY SHERBONDY** is an artist, graphic designer, and owner of the online store lindsayletters.com, where she sells hand-lettered prints, canvases, and other goodies. Lindsay took her first calligraphy class when she was ten and has been lettering through life ever since. She lives in Sun Prairie, Wisconsin, with her super-weird, super-hot, super-smart youth pastor husband Dugan and their best-kids-ever tiny humans, Phoenix Brave (one year) and Eva Love (five years). When she's not lettering or painting or forgetting her keys, she loves being with her friends and family, exploring antique malls and the outdoors, and cluttering her van with half-full cups of iced coffee.

*to see & purchase lindsay's work, check out* **LINDSAYLETTERS.COM**

## *two tiny tips for enjoying this book:*

**1. START WITH PRAYER.** Even if it only lasts for sixty seconds. Before you open this book up, just hold out your hands and say something like this: "Lord, I commit this time to You. I love You. Please speak to me. I offer this time and what I create to You as my humble worship. Thank You for creating me in Your image, and for creating me to create. Amen."

**2. HAVE SO MUCH FUN!!!** Do not be afraid to mess up. Color outside the lines, color inside the lines, take notes in the margins, use colors or just use that ballpoint pen you found on the desk at the hotel. In the words of Cher Horowitz: *WHAT. EVER.* The only way you could possibly mess up this book is if you're afraid to mess it up. My humble advice? Don't wait until a good time to start. Don't put this little coloring book on a "someday maybe" pedestal for when you have "time." Time is a myth. You'll never have it. Start today. If you *hate* the page, you can always rip it out. If you *love* the page, keep it here—or frame that puppy and show everyone you know! Either way, I'd love to walk with you on this journey!

〰 **TAG #COLORSWEETERTHANHONEY on Instagram, Facebook, and Twitter. Let's get the Interwebs swirling with pretty pictures of God's Word—made even sweeter by your attention to it and love for it!**

〰 Follow Lindsay on Instagram at @lindsay_letters.

Also, check out **LINDSAYLETTERS.COM/SWEETERTHANHONEY** for inspiration, videos and more goodies and surprises!

BUT NOW, THIS IS WHAT THE LORD SAYS—HE WHO CREATED YOU,
JACOB, HE WHO FORMED YOU, ISRAEL: "DO NOT FEAR, FOR I HAVE
REDEEMED YOU; I HAVE SUMMONED YOU BY NAME; YOU ARE MINE."

*ISAIAH 43:1, NIV*

## FOOD FOR Thought

*We know that colors are important to God.*
**He is the Great Artist**, as demonstrated by the incredible thought
and detail He put into creation. From brilliant stones to the
most intricate orchids, from sprawling sunsets to the diverse way
He painted insects, animals, and people.

The Lord could have created a grayscale world, but He didn't,
and it's because He knows that color is important. It means
something and **does something to our spirits**. In the same way
that yellow might bring us energy and blue might bring us peace,
we are intentional in the colors we choose—whether we realize
it or not. And so is God!

Do you have some favorite colors you'd like to use in your book?
Take the next few pages to create swatches of those colors.
Reference these pages and draw inspiration from them
as you need to.

AND THEY HAMMERED OUT GOLD LEAF, AND HE CUT IT INTO THREADS
TO WORK INTO THE BLUE AND PURPLE AND THE SCARLET YARNS,
AND INTO THE FINE TWINED LINEN, IN SKILLED DESIGN.

*EXODUS 39:3, ESV*

# these colors make me feel JOYFUL!

Color name

these colors make
me feel restful

I WILL PRAISE YOU, FOR I AM FEARFULLY AND WONDERFULLY
MADE; MARVELOUS ARE YOUR WORKS,
AND THAT MY SOUL KNOWS VERY WELL.

*PSALM 139:14, NKJV*

SO GOD CREATED HUMAN BEINGS IN HIS OWN IMAGE.
IN THE IMAGE OF GOD HE CREATED THEM; MALE AND FEMALE
HE CREATED THEM.

*GENESIS 1:27, NLT*

Thank you for making me & so wonderfully complex! Your workmanship is Marvelous—HOW WELL I know it.

PSALM 139:14

**FOOD FOR Thought**

*Psalm 23* has been one of the verses I've clung to most in my adult life. In this psalm, I think the psalmist, David, inadvertently reminds us of the nurturing character of our God. **When I read, "He leads me beside quiet waters," I picture a strong God, taking me by the hand and walking with me.** Calming me with every step, His grasp firm and gentle. And then He asks me to sit down. ***"SIT?! NOW?!"*** I ask. *"Yes, daughter. Sit. Hear the babble of the brook or the waves chasing up to the shore. Remember me. Focus on me. Breathe."* And then the best part of the verse: the "restore" part. Yes, yes, yes.

**In our lives, most often, these "quiet waters" need to be figurative.** We can't always get to a beautiful body of water to nourish our souls. But we *can* create these quiet waters in any scenario. I believe that our mighty and creative God can restore souls on the subway or in the classroom or in a hut or at the park or in a hotel room. **However, it is up to us to allow Him to.** To place our minds and hearts in a ready posture for Him to take us by the hand and lead us to this restorative space. Any day, any time, wherever you are. **Would you make your heart and hand available for the leading?**

HE MAKES ME TO LIE DOWN IN GREEN PASTURES; HE LEADS ME BESIDE THE STILL WATERS. HE RESTORES MY SOUL; HE LEADS ME IN THE PATHS OF RIGHTEOUSNESS FOR HIS NAME'S SAKE.

*PSALM 23:2-3, NKJV*

TASTE AND SEE THAT THE LORD IS GOOD;
BLESSED IS THE ONE WHO TAKES REFUGE IN HIM.

*PSALM 34:82, NIV*

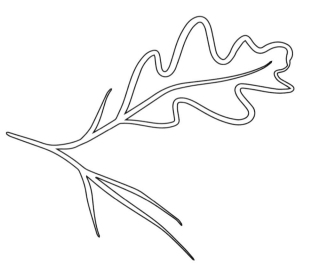

In Psalm 46:10, as well as in Exodus 14:14,
*God is calling us to "be still"—to simply rest in*
*His presence, and take heart in knowing that*
*the Master of the Universe is at work on your behalf.*

Are you in a season of striving? Worry? Restlessness?
Busyness? As you create on this next page, prayerfully ask
God what He is asking you to **offer up to Him** so that you
might be able to be still. Ask Him to help you.
His yoke is easy and His burden is light (Matthew 11:30)
and He wants nothing more than for you to take comfort
in knowing that He's got you in the palm of
His hand (Isaiah 49:16).

**BE STILL, AND KNOW THAT I AM GOD.
I WILL BE EXALTED AMONG THE NATIONS,
I WILL BE EXALTED IN THE EARTH!**

*PSALM 46:10, ESV*

When I get tired of waiting on God, I figure that He has forgotten me. That the vision He gave me wasn't real. That the prayers I am praying aren't being heard. Or worse yet, He doesn't care. And so instead of waiting at the foot of the mountain, expectant, I start going to work myself. I start seeking other answers, other plans, other things that could satisfy me or give me the answers that I want. I start creating new gods.

How many times have I missed the miracle because I rushed the answer?

*ASHLEY McNARY*
*Exodus: God's Relentless Pursuit of Us*

CAST ALL YOUR ANXIETY ON HIM BECAUSE HE CARES FOR YOU.

*1 PETER 5:7*

AND IF GOD CARES SO WONDERFULLY FOR WILDFLOWERS
THAT ARE HERE TODAY AND THROWN INTO THE FIRE TOMORROW,
HE WILL CERTAINLY CARE FOR YOU.
WHY DO YOU HAVE SO LITTLE FAITH?

*MATTHEW 6:30, NLT*

ARE YOU TIRED? WORN OUT? BURNED OUT ON RELIGION?
COME TO ME. GET AWAY WITH ME AND YOU'LL RECOVER YOUR
LIFE. I'LL SHOW YOU HOW TO TAKE A REAL REST. WALK WITH ME
AND WORK WITH ME—WATCH HOW I DO IT. LEARN THE UNFORCED
RHYTHMS OF GRACE. I WON'T LAY ANYTHING HEAVY OR ILL-
FITTING ON YOU. KEEP COMPANY WITH ME AND YOU'LL LEARN
TO LIVE FREELY AND LIGHTLY.

*MATTHEW 11:29-30, MSG*

I will refresh the weary and satisfy the faint

JEREMIAH 31:25

HOW PRECIOUS ARE YOUR THOUGHTS ABOUT ME, O GOD.
THEY CANNOT BE NUMBERED!
I CAN'T EVEN COUNT THEM;
THEY OUTNUMBER THE GRAINS OF SAND!
AND WHEN I WAKE UP,
YOU ARE STILL WITH ME!

PSALM 139:17-18, NLT

### *Do you feel "satisfied"?*

Generally, to feel satisfied I feel like I need a doughnut.
Or mac'n'cheese. It feels much easier to try to satisfy myself with
whatever I can get my hands on, instead of with the Lord.
I'm bummed? I buy lipstick. Stressed? I eat my feelings. Lonely?
Netflix to the rescue. Happy? Also with the eating and the lipstick and
the Netflix. Feeling like I want to punch someone? For a run I go.
And then there's the proverbial coffee-shaped hole in my heart. (Don't
judge me, tea people. I see you out there and I also know your ways.)

**God wants us to be fully satisfied in Him alone.** I'm not suggesting
that we not eat when we're hungry or that we find positive ways to
manage our stress. But man, how I wish that the Lord was the first
place I turned to. That, out of habit, He would be the fight in my
physiological fight-or-flight response. That I'd invite Him along with
me on my run or during my coffee break.

As you create on this next page, **ask the Lord to come along with you.**
Ask Him to teach you how to be fully satisfied in Him. To turn to Him
first, and then take Him with you as you proceed.

I will be fully satisfied as with the richest of foods with singing lips my mouth will praise you

PSALM 63:5

As a DEER longs for a stream of cool water, so I long for you, o God

PSALM 42:1

SOW RIGHTEOUSNESS FOR YOURSELVES, REAP THE FRUIT OF
UNFAILING LOVE, AND BREAK UP YOUR UNPLOWED GROUND;
FOR IT IS TIME TO SEEK THE LORD, UNTIL HE COMES AND
SHOWERS HIS RIGHTEOUSNESS ON YOU.

*HOSEA 10:12, NIV*

IN THIS MANNER, THEREFORE, PRAY:

OUR FATHER IN HEAVEN,
HALLOWED BE YOUR NAME.
YOUR KINGDOM COME.
YOUR WILL BE DONE
ON EARTH AS IT IS IN HEAVEN.
GIVE US THIS DAY OUR DAILY BREAD.
AND FORGIVE US OUR DEBTS,
AS WE FORGIVE OUR DEBTORS.
AND DO NOT LEAD US INTO TEMPTATION,
BUT DELIVER US FROM THE EVIL ONE.
FOR YOURS IS THE KINGDOM AND THE
POWER AND THE GLORY FOREVER.
AMEN.

*MATTHEW 6:9-15, NKJV*

When peace like a river, attendeth my way, When sorrow like sea billows roll Whatever my lot, thou has taught me, to say, It is well, it is well, With my soul

You turn my mourning into joyful dancing

PSALM 30:11

**"Selah" is a Hebrew word** that is used seventy-four times in the Bible, mostly in the Psalms, and three times in Habakkuk. Scholars aren't in total agreement about what the word means, but based on where it appears and the frequency of it, we can be pretty sure that "*selah*" is a musical term, indicating a breath or pause before continuing.

Say it out loud, slowly: "*say-lah.*" **Doesn't it just sound like a breath?** The word in and of itself almost forces you to slow down in its very phoenetics. And so, as directed, that's what we'll do on this next page (and hopefully throughout this book). Take a breath. A pause. Reflect on the worship we just experienced and the worship to come. **Let the blessing of your worship— through creating—wash over you like beautiful music.**

WHO IS THIS KING OF GLORY? THE LORD OF HOSTS
HE IS THE KING OF GLORY. *Selah*
P S A L M   2 4 : 9 - 1 0 ,   N K J V

One thing I
LORD, this
that I may
house of the
days of my
on the beauty
and to seek Him

ask from the only do I seek: dwell in the LORD all the life, to gaze of the LORD in His temple.

PSALM 27:4

TURN THOU US UNTO THEE, O LORD, AND WE SHALL BE TURNED;
RENEW OUR DAYS AS OF OLD.

*LAMENTATIONS 5:21, KJV*

breathe new breath

The world will tell you how to live, if you let it. Don't let it. Take up your space. Raise your voice. Sing your song. This is your chance to make or remake a life that thrills you.

*S H A U N A   N I E Q U I S T*
*Present Over Perfect: Leaving Behind Frantic for a Simpler,*
*More Soulful Way of Living*

Praise God
from whom all
Blessings flow
Praise Him all
creatures here below
Praise Him above
Ye heavenly hosts
Praise Father, Son
and Holy Ghost

I WILL NEVER FORGET THIS AWFUL TIME,
AS I GRIEVE OVER MY LOSS.
YET I STILL DARE TO HOPE
WHEN I REMEMBER THIS:
THE FAITHFUL LOVE OF THE LORD NEVER ENDS!
HIS MERCIES NEVER CEASE.
GREAT IS HIS FAITHFULNESS;
HIS MERCIES BEGIN AFRESH EACH MORNING.

*LAMENTATIONS 3:20-23, NLT*

Light is sweet how pleasant to see a NEW DAY Dawning

ECCLESIASTES 11:7

## FOOD FOR Thought

I was never super excited about reading the Old Testament. I wanted to hurry up and get to the Jesus part! But I forced myself to start there, because my mother-in-law and my best friend are both obsessed with the Old Testament, and because I knew that I would understand even better how cool the New Testament is after first reading through the Old.

What most sticks out to me, as I read through those pages, is that *people asked things of the Lord, and He graciously delivered.* He gave Moses a partner, the Israelites a second chance, Gideon a sign, Ruth a family, Hannah a son. He gave wisdom to Solomon, favor to Esther, protection to Daniel, success to Nehemiah. What does this show me? That **God hears us, and God answers.** Not always in the ways we want, but sometimes He really does answer in the ways we want! (He's even changed His mind as the result of prayer!)

**And so we can, with confidence, come boldly before this throne of God.** Tell Him what's on your mind and what's in your heart. What are you longing for? Do not be afraid to ask. God wants desperately to be involved in your life. Start here: get on your knees. Thank Him for who He is and what He has done, repent, and then ask Him for what your soul is aching for. Whether it's actually—for the love of all things holy—*finally* finding a perfectly ripe avocado at the store when you need one, or if it's the deep, deep desires that are constantly tugging at your heart. Bring it *all* to Him. **And then wait upon the Lord** (Psalm 27:14).

And to Him be all the honor and glory if we're blessed to see our prayers answered in the ways we so deeply desire.

DELIGHT YOURSELF IN THE LORD,
AND HE WILL GIVE YOU THE DESIRES OF YOUR HEART.

*PSALM 37:4, ESV*

SO LET'S DO IT—FULL OF BELIEF, CONFIDENT THAT WE'RE
PRESENTABLE INSIDE AND OUT. LET'S KEEP A FIRM GRIP ON THE
PROMISES THAT KEEP US GOING. HE ALWAYS KEEPS HIS WORD.
LET'S SEE HOW INVENTIVE WE CAN BE IN ENCOURAGING LOVE AND
HELPING OUT, NOT AVOIDING WORSHIPING TOGETHER AS SOME DO
BUT SPURRING EACH OTHER ON, ESPECIALLY AS WE SEE THE
BIG DAY APPROACHING.

*HEBREWS 10:23-25, MSG*

I will deliver you from the wilderness and take you to a land flowing with milk and honey

EXODUS 3:17

My friend Mike Breaux coined this phrase, and it's as fresh and inspiring in my mind today as the first time I heard it in church that Sunday. ***Re-wallpaper your mind with the word of God.*** Every day, thousands and thousands of words get tossed at us. Sometimes these are sweet words—affirmation from a friend, accolades from a coworker, loving words from your spouse or kids. Other times, these words may not be so sweet. Words like "too much." Too thin, too fat, too busy, too young, too old. Words like "not enough." Not good enough, not smart enough, not pretty enough, not educated enough. Yuck. You will probably get loads of bad advice in your life: heaps of unsolicited guidance about dating or marriage or parenting or school or work. Cutting through the clutter of all the noise can feel nearly impossible some days. Who is right? What am I? What am I not? And where to find the truth?

**The Truth, friends, can only be found in God's word.** Have you ever taken down old wallpaper? It's a hot mess. A gross, sticky mess. Actually, putting up fresh wallpaper isn't much of a picnic, either. But this is the hard work we must do. Get messy. Put some elbow grease into it. Pour Truth over that crumbling, crackling wallpaper and watch the hurt and lies and negativity fall away with every scrape of scripture and every nod to Jesus. It won't be easy to re-wallpaper your mind. A good place to start is to not let the old stuff pile up into layers. It will only be harder to scrape off later. Take every bit of junk and replace it with Truth. **Every day, all day.**

This is hard work, but it's work worth doing. As you color this next page,
I pray that you can visualize the Holy Spirit doing work in you.
Tackling that old wallpaper with every pencil/pen stroke you make.
**Making a clean slate, primed and ready for the goodness of God.**

re-Wallpaper your mind with the word of god

The Bible talks about our need to strip away the old and put on the new—kind of like re-wallpapering our minds. "Don't copy the behavior and customs of this world, but let God transform you into a new person by changing the way you think" (Romans 12:2). When you know what God says and renew your mind daily to the truth, you start to think differently about God, about yourself, about others, and about life. Every day, as you re-wallpaper your mind with the life-changing words of God, our perspective starts to change.

*MIKE BREAUX*
*Identity Theft: Reclaiming Who God Created You to Be*

GOD's word is better than a diamond set between emeralds... Better than Strawberries in the Spring better than red, RIPE Strawberries. psalm 19:10

gracious words are a honeycomb sweet to the soul and healing to the bones

PROVERBS 16:24

*the Lips of the RIGHTEOUS nourish many*

PROVERBS 10:21a

### *Have you ever felt broken?*

Like you left a huge mess behind in the place or places you came from?
I know I have. Lots. Lots of decisions that ended in piles of rubble, lots of
people hurt because of my choices, lots of ashes. Perhaps the ruins at your
feet weren't because of something you did at all, but because of something
done to you or to someone you love? Can we pray for this?

I'm not of the belief that everything happens for a reason. I *am* of the
belief that the Holy Spirit works within our mess—creatively and intensely
working to turn what is broken into something beautiful. Isn't that an
incredible thought? There is nothing that God cannot redeem
(Romans 8:28).

However, there is a catch, and it's this: **You cannot cling tight to the ashes.**
You must come to Him with open hands and simply say, "Lord, this is what
I have. This is all I have. I know it cannot ever be beautiful without You.
Please, do Your good work within me, work within these ashes.
I love You, and I give You all the glory, now and forever."

*A M E N*

**God uses broken things. It takes broken soil to produce a crop,
broken clouds to give rain, broken grain to give bread, broken bread
to give strength. It is the broken alabaster box that gives forth perfume.
It is Peter, weeping bitterly, who returns to greater power than ever.**

*V A N C E   H A V N E R*

ISAIAH 61:3

There is such a love, a love that creates value in what is loved. There is
a love that turns rag dolls into priceless treasures. There is a love that
fastens itself onto ragged little creatures, for reasons that no one could
ever quite figure out, and makes them precious and valued beyond
calculation. This is love beyond reason. This is the love of God.

**JOHN ORTBERG**
*Love Beyond Reason: Moving God's Love from Your Head to Your Hearts*

FOR YOU HAVE BEEN BOUGHT WITH A PRICE; THEREFORE BE GLORIFYING
GOD WITH YOUR BODY AND WITH YOUR SPIRIT, WHICH ARE GOD'S.

*1 CORINTHIANS 6:20*

*Aramaic Bible in Plain English*

AND HE WHO WAS SEATED ON THE THRONE SAID,
"BEHOLD, I AM MAKING ALL THINGS NEW." ALSO HE SAID, "WRITE
THIS DOWN, FOR THESE WORDS ARE TRUSTWORTHY AND TRUE."

REVELATION 21:5, ESV

**Sometimes, I admit, I totally forget about the Holy Spirit.**
Jesus I remember. I am so thankful for His love and sacrifice and for
His nearness to me. God, the Almighty Creator of the Universe? Yep,
I remember Him, too. But I often forget that when I became a believer in
Jesus Christ and surrendered my life to the Lord, the Holy Spirit took up
residence in me. In my body, in my heart. That means that the same power
Jesus used to calm the waves and heal the sick and raise from the dead
(Romans 8:11) is in me. Are you a follower of Jesus?
**Then it's in you, too.**

Do I even tap into one tiny smidgen of that power on a daily basis? I mean,
if I'm honest, it actually kind of scares me. **But we need it.** That's why He
allows us to have it—right? We need the power of the Holy Spirit in us
because the truth is that this life isn't always easy. For some of us, actually,
it's never easy. And in the words of one of my favorite philosophers—
Spider-Man's uncle—**"With great power comes great responsibility."**

We need the power of the Holy Spirit in us to do this life well, to walk in
a cadence that even resembles that of Jesus. He has made you strong, because
**HE is strong, and He is Mighty in YOU.**

*READ   MORE in a letter from Paul* → **EPHESIANS 1:11-23**

I have made you strong. ♡

HE BRINGS FORTH food from the EARTH WINE THAT Gladdens human hearts OIL TO make their faces shine and BREAD THAT SUSTAINS human hearts

PSALM 104:14

HE HAS MADE EVERYTHING BEAUTIFUL IN ITS TIME. HE HAS ALSO
SET ETERNITY IN THE HUMAN HEART; YET NO ONE CAN FATHOM
WHAT GOD HAS DONE FROM BEGINNING TO END.

*ECCLESIASTES 3:11, NIV*

*I'm not sure what it is about the word "flourish" that makes it feel extravagant.* Fancy. Like a flourishing life would look like a life wrapped in a feather boa, arms open wide and ready to burst into jazz-hands or a glittering selfie at any moment. Not bad, just a far cry from the yoga pants and mashed-up baby food situation I have going on at the present moment. Maybe you're not covered in pulverized peaches like me but still don't feel all that jazz-hands-y nonetheless. To flourish seems just about as attainable becoming a butterfly.

Well here's the thing: **We don't need to have a fancy life to flourish.** We don't need to have what we might classify as a big, exciting life to flourish. **To flourish simply means to be able to grow into your fullest self.** Your best possible self. In John 10:10, Jesus says, "But I have come that they may have life, and have it to the full." What does this mean? It means that if we do this life, if we live out Jesus's way (love others, love ourselves, be obedient to His practices and His truths, and seek Him above all else), we will find life there. Full, abundant life. *A free life.* This is the life your Father wants for you, **so much so that He gave His Son for it.**

What's **one thing** you can turn over to the Lord today that would bring you one step closer to flourishing in Him?

BUT I AM LIKE AN OLIVE TREE FLOURISHING IN THE HOUSE OF GOD;
I TRUST IN GOD'S UNFAILING LOVE FOR EVER AND EVER.

*PSALM 52:8, NIV*

But I am like an olive tree flourishing in the house of God; I trust in God's unfailing love forever

FOR WE ARE GOD'S MASTERPIECE. HE HAS CREATED US ANEW
IN CHRIST JESUS, SO WE CAN DO THE GOOD THINGS HE PLANNED
FOR US LONG AGO.

*EPHESIANS 2:10, NLT*

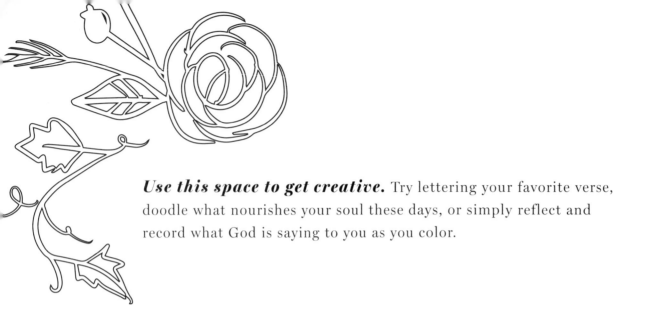

**Use this space to get creative.** Try lettering your favorite verse, doodle what nourishes your soul these days, or simply reflect and record what God is saying to you as you color.

## acknowledgements

So much thanks go to Katy Hamilton, the team at HarperOne, and Jenni Burke—thank you for allowing me the opportunity to create this book with you, and for holding my hand and walking along with me down this new publishing path. It's pretty here along this road with you guys, and I love what we've created together.

A million hugs to Jess Connolly, Whitney English, Shauna Niequist, Emily Ley, and Lara Casey for being there for me in the middle of it all—for taking the time to respond to a panicked text, to dream, to raise your hand and say "me too" right along with me, and for modeling what it means to be a mama and simultaneously run a creative business with integrity in the name of loving others and loving Jesus.

Thanks to my Heartland Rockford small group. What an anomaly of friendship for the perfect time in our lives. Your many, many years of encouragement ring on in my ears and continue to fuel my efforts. To Sherri and Mark for the initial opportunity to work and grow under your leadership and wisdom, and for your continued support. To Casey for believing in me in ways I didn't believe in myself.

To Laura—you are way more than my photographer or my friend from Kansas City. You complete me. Your love of Jesus and people and appreciation of beauty is an influence in most everything I make, and I simply couldn't do it without you. From conception to the finished photo, my work is better because you are a part of it.

To Em and Jenna and Sara—for opening up your lives and inviting me in with open arms and humor and love. To Sasha for loving E & P (and us!) so incredibly well. To Ran and Ty for being family. To Drea, Chrissy, Steph, and Ashley. You are the best best best friends a girl could ask for. Ash—there simply aren't words. Your wisdom and support and love and ideas and vision and cooking and packing and stories and emojis and ministry and just . . . everything. I'm the luckiest.

To Mom, Martin, Dad and Mary—thank you thank you for your unconditional love and support! To Sharon/M—you are an inspirational gem in the life of whomever you meet. Your constant prayer and encouragement mean the world. To Eva Love—you are a beautiful, dazzling, sparkling human. You are the most creative person I have ever met, and to get to see the world through your eyes allows me to know Jesus more. I love getting to be your mama! To Phoenix Brave—you are the best baby in the whole world and I literally want to eat your squishy face. To D—thanks for so many things. But regarding my work, thank you for encouraging me to be my truest self. For not allowing the practicality of the non-best parts of me get in the way of what you knew the best parts would allow me to become in the name of Jesus. And thank you for the huge sacrifice you make every day to allow me to pursue my passion. I love you so, so much.

And last, but certainly not least—you. Thank you for picking up this book, and for getting this far. If I could pray for one thing for you, I would pray that deep within your spirit, you would know that the Lord believes that you are worthy of love, care, and the honor of experiencing and enjoying the beauty He has created—beginning with yourself.